Mary and

of Guadalupe, Lourdes and Fatima

Written by
Dr. Elaine Murray Stone

Edited by
Joseph Schiller

Regina Press
New York

THE REGINA PRESS
10 Hub Drive
Melville, New York

Printed in Hong Kong.

ISBN: 0-88271-139-3

Mary

$\mathcal{T}$he woman who would eventually become known as the Blessed Virgin Mary was born over 2,000 years ago in a small Judean town named Nazareth. Her parents were Anne and Joachim. We are told that her father, Joachim, had wanted a child so badly that he once went into the desert where he fasted and prayed for forty days. In time his prayers were apparently answered because his wife, Anne, did give birth to a beautiful baby girl whom they named Mary.

Tradition tells us that Mary grew up in Nazareth with no special honor or distinction. And while we know little about her daily life as a child, it was most probably one of simplicity, poverty, and hard work.

In the middle of her teenage years, after she had been promised in marriage to a man named Joseph, Mary was visited by an angel who said to her, "Peace be with you! The Lord is with you, and has greatly blessed you!"

Since the angel's appearance caused Mary to feel fear, the angel said to her, "Don't be afraid, Mary, because God has been gracious to you. In fact, in the months ahead, you will become pregnant and will give birth to a son, and you will name him Jesus. Your Son will be great and will be called the Son of the Most High God." Although she really did not understand everything the angel was telling her, she

did find the angel's words to be somewhat reassuring. We are told that before the angel left, Mary responded by saying, "I am the Lord's servant. May it happen to me as you have said."

In the months which followed, Mary began to better understand how her life would be changed. Only time would reveal the full impact of the angel's invitation and her own answer, "Yes, let it be done."

Not long before her son was to be born, the Roman emperor, Augustus, decreed that a census had to be taken throughout all the lands under Roman rule. People living in towns and villages where they had not been born had to return to their home towns and give the government the necessary census information. Since Mary was married to Joseph, they had to make a journey to Bethlehem, the town in which Joseph's ancestors had lived.

Shortly after arriving in Bethlehem, Mary gave birth to her son whom she named Jesus, as the angel had requested.

The Bible tells us that after the birth of Jesus, angels appeared to a group of shepherds and told them that a baby had been born in Bethlehem. This child would grow up to become the Savior whom the Jewish people had been promised many generations earlier. Upon hearing this good news, the shepherds hurried to Bethlehem were they found the baby lying in a manger. Some time later, Mary, Joseph, and Jesus were also visited by three wise men who lived many miles east of where Jesus had been born.

In the months which followed, Mary and Joseph took Jesus to Egypt where they lived for some time, avoiding a persecution ordered by Herod, a Roman governor who feared that a Jewish savior would threaten his authority. When Herod finally died, the three returned to Nazareth where Mary and Joseph had previously lived.

When Jesus was in his early thirties, he began preaching, teaching, and healing, both in Nazareth and in the neighboring communities. During this time, the Bible gives some mention of his mother Mary, but not enough is said to give a very detailed description of her life on earth. When her son, Jesus, was crucified, Mary stood at the foot of his cross. She later gathered with Jesus' disciples after his resurrection. We might assume that Jesus and Mary visited during the time between his resurrection and ascension, but neither historical records nor the Bible record any of these more personal visits.

After Jesus' ascension, there is some good indication that Mary was cared for in Ephesus, Turkey, by one of Jesus' apostles, John. The remainder of her earthly life was lived as it was begun, in a rather quiet and uneventful existence. Or at least that is what one assumes since nothing further had been written about her life. And while the details of her death have also been lost to recorded history, the Christian community has always believed

that upon her earthly death, she was taken to heaven in both body and soul.

For most ordinary men and women born into this world, death is where the recorded history of their life ends. But the Blessed Virgin Mary, the Mother of Jesus, is an exception.

In the hundreds of years which have passed since her earthly death, there have been numerous accounts of new earthly visits which have become known as apparitions. Some of them have been officially accepted as verifiably true, while many others have not been officially accepted.

Three of the most widely known apparitions occurred within the past five hundred years in Mexico, France, and Portugal. In time, the specific place of each apparition provided new names for the Blessed Virgin Mary. The apparition in Mexico gave Our Lady the title "Our Lady of Guadalupe." The apparition in France gave her the title "Our Lady of Lourdes" and the apparition in Portugal gave her the title "Our Lady of Fatima." Dr. Elaine Murray Stone tells the stories of these apparitions.

Joseph Schiller,
Editor

Our Lady of Guadalupe

*F*ew people who live in the Americas are not familiar with the year 1492. It is the year when Christopher Columbus assumed that he had discovered a previously unknown part of this earth. Actually, the two vast American continents had been discovered many thousands of years earlier, but word of this discovery had never quite reached the peoples of Europe who believed they lived in the center of the civilized world.

Once word of this so-called discovery spread across Europe, plans for the conquest of the new lands began to unfold, and it took little time for those plans to be turned into action.

In just a few short years, ships loaded with fortune-seekers were heading for the Americas in hopes of finding gold and all sorts of other treasures. Unfortunately, most of the Europeans had little interest in trading with the native people they found. The European conquest of the American continent had begun with great enthusiasm, and its completion came much sooner than many would have expected.

Within only a few decades, the country which we now call Mexico was conquered by Hernando Cortez, and both the Spanish culture and the Catholic religion was introduced and taught to the native peoples whom we now

call the Aztecs.

One of the earliest Christian "converts" was an Aztec man named Juan Diego. Juan, who had been eighteen years old when Columbus first "discovered" America, lived in a place named Cuantitlan, close to the city we now call Mexico City. Like his fellow Aztec brothers and sisters, he was a simple, powerless and uneducated peasant farmer.

One day in 1531, Juan was on his way to attend Mass as had become his custom after accepting the new Christian religion.

When he passed Tepeyac Hill, he heard birds singing. Then a soft voice called saying, "Juan come up here." Juan didn't want to go. At the top of the hill were the ruins of an Aztec temple. The priest had told Juan not to have anything to do with the old religion.

But the woman's sweet voice called louder, "Come up Juan, I have something to tell you." Juan was curious. He began to climb the steep hill. The bird's singing and the sweet voice drew him higher and higher.

Suddenly at the top of the hill, Juan saw a beautiful lady. All around her were golden rays. She was dressed in a blue cape dotted with stars. Juan fell to his knees in wonder.

Then the maiden told him, "I am the Virgin Mary, the Mother of God. I desire that a chapel be built here. There I will hear your people's troubles and relieve their sufferings."

The vision added, "Go to the Bishop in Mexico City

and tell him everything you have seen and heard." Amazed by the beauty of the vision, Juan replied, "Yes, my Lady, I will do everything you asked." Then he scrambled down the hill and rushed toward the city.

At the Bishop's house, he knocked on the door. A servant saw it was only a poor Indian standing on the stoop. He refused to open the door.

Juan knocked again. "I must see the Bishop," he called out. "I bring him an important message." This time the servant opened the door and led Juan to the Bishop's office.

Juan told the Bishop everything he had seen. He described the beautiful lady of Tepeyac Hill who appeared to him. Then he gave the Bishop the Vision's message. "She asked you to build a chapel in her honor."

The Spanish Bishop found it difficult to believe the Holy Virgin would appear to a poor Indian. He asked Juan about his life and faith. Finally the Bishop said, "Ask the Lady for a sign, then I will believe and carry out her wishes."

Juan was disappointed. He hurried home where he discovered his uncle was sick and near death. The old man begged Juan to bring a priest. Juan left before dawn. Hoping to reach the church faster, he walked around the opposite side of Tepeyac Hill.

Suddenly the Virgin Mary appeared again. Golden lights surrounded her. A cherub lay at her feet. She seemed to float above the rough, brown grass.

In the same sweet voice the vision asked, "Where are you going, my son?" Bowing low, Juan explained, "I'm hurrying to bring a priest to my dying uncle — to hear his last confession." "Do not worry," the Lady told Juan. "At this very moment your uncle is completely healed."

Amazed and grateful Juan thanked the beautiful lady. Then he told her, "Yesterday I spoke to the Bishop. He asked that you give him a sign. Then he will believe and build the chapel you asked for."

The Lady told Juan, "Climb to the top of Tepeyac Hill. There you will find many roses. Gather them and bring them back to me." Juan did as the Lady requested. Even though it was winter, he found many bushes covered with beautiful red roses.

Juan wore a tilma, a rough cape woven of cactus fiber. He laid the cape on the ground and filled it with the blooming roses. Then he returned to show the Lady. The Holy Virgin rearranged the flowers and tied the corners of the tilma behind Juan's neck.

"Now go," she said. "Take these roses to the Bishop as the sign he requested. Then remind him to carry out my wishes and build a chapel here to honor me."

Juan hurried off to the Bishop's house. "I have a sign for the Bishop," he told the servant. This time he was taken directly to the Bishop's office. Juan said to the Bishop, "The Lady told me to pick roses at the top of Tepeyac Hill.

She ordered me to bring them to you as a sign of her appearance." With these words Juan opened his tilma spilling dozens of huge red roses at the Bishop's feet.

But the Bishop's eyes were not on the roses. He was staring at Juan's empty tilma. For on it was a portrait of the Lady exactly as Juan had described her. All the people in the room dropped to their knees before the miraculous image of Mary, the Holy Mother of God.

Finally convinced, the Bishop ordered a chapel at Tepayac Hill built in the Virgin's honor. There many miracles began to be reported. Thousands of sick people came to pray in the chapel and claimed to be healed. In 1709, a great church was built to replace the small chapel. Juan's tilma was placed above the altar for all to see. The picture on it became known as The Virgin of Guadalupe.

When the ancient church began sinking into the ground, an even larger basilica was built in 1975 to replace it. Now 450 years old, the picture of Our Lady of Guadalupe is as bright as when it was new. The tilma is in perfect condition.

Juan Diego died in 1548 and is buried at Tepeyac Hill. In 1990, he was recognized as one of the Saints of God and beautified in Rome by Pope John Paul II. He was canonized on July 31, 2002. His feast day is December 9.

Our Lady of Lourdes

*I*n a small town in southern France, at the foot of the Pyrenees Mountains, on the seventh day of January, 1844, a baby girl was born to Francois Soubirous and Louise Casterot. She was named Bernadette. On the day of her birth, few people in the world had ever heard of the town in which she was born. However, that would change. Today, pilgrims travel to Lourdes from every corner of the globe.

One winter day in 1858, Bernadette's mother sent her to gather wood for the stove. Bernadette's sister Toinette and friend Jeanne went with her.

The girls walked through the woods, picked up branches and sticks until they came to the River Gave. Toinette and Jeanne waded through the icy water to the other side. But Bernadette held back.

"Come on over," the girls called. Finally Bernadette took off her shoes and bravely followed the others across the stream.

Continuing on their way, the girls came to Massabielle, the city dump where garbage lay everywhere.

On the right stood a high cliff. In the rock was a cave or grotto, usually used by shepherds for shelter during storms.

Bernadette walked toward the grotto. But suddenly she stopped and dropped to her knees. The young girl stared up at a niche high in the rock.

Then she took a rosary from her pocket and began to pray. "What's wrong?" asked her sister. Bernadette continued to stare at the niche and pray. Toinette was worried. "Get up, Bernadette" she said. "We can't keep our mother waiting."

Bernadette stood up. Carrying their bundles of firewood, the three girls hurried home.

On the walk back home Bernadette explained what happened at Massabielle. "I saw a beautiful Lady," she told them. "We recited the rosary together."

When the girls arrived home they found Madame Soubirous very angry. "Where have you been all this time?" she asked crossly. "I need this wood to start dinner."

"Bernadette saw a Lady," tattled her sister. "What Lady?" asked their mother. "Oh Mother, the Lady was so beautiful!" exclaimed Bernadette. "She wore a long white gown tied at the waist with a blue ribbon. There were golden rays all round her and yellow roses on her feet."

Madame Soubirous' face turned red. "Don't lie to me Bernadette," she threatened. "Stay away from Massabielle! Do you understand?" "Yes Mama," Bernadette answered softly.

But the pull of the beautiful vision was too hard for her to resist. Three days later Bernadette started out early for the grotto. A gang of boys followed, making fun of her.

Arriving at the grotto, Bernadette knelt down, keeping

her eyes on the niche where she had seen the Lady. The young girl prayed so hard she fell to the ground in a trance. All the boys screamed for help.

Nicolou, a nearby miller, heard the commotion and came running. He carried the unconscious girl to his mill. When Bernadette finally woke up, Nicolou and his wife took her back home.

When Madame Soubirous saw her pale daughter too weak to stand, she became upset. Once again she ordered Bernadette never again to visit the grotto.

The Mayor of Lourdes heard about Bernadette's vision. He visited the Soubirous' one-room home. He ordered Bernadette not to go to Massabielle.

The police chief and the local priest spoke to Bernadette too. Several people thought perhaps she was having a mental breakdown. They sent Dr. Dozous to examine Bernadette. He found her perfectly normal.

Soon after Bernadette felt better, two important ladies of Lourdes offered to go with Bernadette to the grotto. Mademoiselle Peyret brought pen and paper to write down whatever the vision said. Madame Millet carried a candle .

After attending an early Mass, the three set out for Massabielle. Arriving at the grotto, Bernadette dropped to her knees. Gazing toward the grotto, Bernadette called out, "Look! There she is." But no one else saw anything.

A huge crowd had followed Bernadette from Lourdes.

The people watched silently as Bernadette spoke with the Lady. The Lady told Bernadette, "Repent and pray for the conversion of sinners." Everyone saw Bernadette kiss the ground in penitence. Then the Lady told Bernadette, "Return here every day for fifteen days."

Bernadette did as the Lady asked. On the sixth visit the Lady told Bernadette, "Drink and wash in the fountain." The girl looked around for water. Bernadette began to dig in the mud below the grotto. Suddenly a trickle of water appeared. Next a stream sprang from the hole.

The crowd watched as Bernadette washed her face in the muddy water. Then she drank it!

Every day huge crowds followed Bernadette to the grotto. On the thirteenth visit to the grotto, the Lady told Bernadette, "I want a chapel built here. Tell the priests to come with a candlelight procession." When Bernadette told the priest, he said, "Ask the Lady who she is."

On March 25 (The Feast of the Annunciation) Bernadette got up early and ran all the way to the grotto. When the beautiful Lady appeared, Bernadette asked, "Who are you?" The Lady answered, "I am the Immaculate Conception." On hearing the vision's reply, Bernadette was confused. She went to the priest. The Father explained the Lady's words meant she was the Virgin Mary, the Queen of Heaven, and the Mother of God!

A great church was built near the grotto. Thousands of

people traveled to Lourdes to pray. Many sick and crippled people came hoping to be healed in the miraculous spring. Many wanted to see Bernadette. She did not like all the fame and went to live in a convent far way. She died there when she was only thirty five.

On December 8, 1933, the Feast of the Immaculate Conception, Bernadette was proclaimed a saint. Every year the Grotto at Lourdes is visited by more and more people. Today it is one of the most popular shrines in the world. Five million people visit Lourdes each year.

Our Lady of Fatima

By all accounts, 1916 was a dark year in human history. World War I was tearing Europe apart, and in Russia, Communism was about to reveal its ugly face. And yet, in a small peasant hamlet, in the center of Portugal, life was being lived much as it had been for many previous centuries. It was slow and uncomplicated. The modern world had little to say to the simple people of Fatima who provided for themselves through manual labor, the maintenance of family gardens, and the herding of sheep, goats, and cows.

On a cool and rainy spring morning in 1916, three of Fatima's children were grazing their sheep and playing in the countryside when suddenly a very bright light appeared before them. They were Lucia dos Santos, age ten, and her cousins: Francisco, eight, and Jacinta, seven, the youngest of the Marto family.

From this light there then emerged what they thought was a young man, whiter than snow, transparent as crystal, and of great beauty. He identified himself to Lucia, Jacinta, and Francisco as the Angel of Peace. He told the children not to be afraid.

The angel then bowed low to the ground and told the children, "Pray this prayer three times: 'My God, I believe,

I adore you. I hope and love you. I ask pardon for those who do not believe, do not adore, do not hope and do not love you.' " Then the angel disappeared.

In the summer and in the fall, the Angel of Peace again appeared to the children. But when winter came, the Angel of Peace did not return.

Then, on May 13, 1917, the three shepherd children led their sheep to the Cova da Iria to graze. It was the same place they had seen the angel.

Suddenly, a flash of light tore through the clear, blue sky. Then a small cloud appeared on the branch of a nearby tree. In that cloud the children saw a beautiful Lady dressed in sparkling white. She held a rosary which looked like pearls. Flashes of light beamed all around her.

The children were frightened. They started to run away. But Lucia told the younger ones to stay. She asked the beautiful Lady, "Where are you from?"

"I come from heaven," replied the Lady. Then Lucia asked, "Why have you come?"

The Lady said, "I want you children to return here on the thirteenth day of each month, for the next six months. I will then tell you who I am and what I want you to do."

Then the Lady drifted off into the sunlight and disappeared.

The children were filled with awe at the vision they had

seen. Lucia wondered if she should tell anyone. Francisco said, "No one will believe us anyway." But little Jacinta told her mother. The story spread through the village.

The Lady had instructed the children to return on June 13. That time they were followed by a crowd all the way to the Cova da Iria. At exactly noon, the Lady appeared. Dazzling flashes of light poured from her outstretched hands.

Lucia asked the Lady, "Will I go to heaven?" The Lady answered, "Francisco and Jacinta will soon be in heaven. But you must stay here to carry out devotion to my Immaculate Heart." (The children saw a vision of the Immaculate Heart.) Then the Lady added, "Continue to come here on the thirteenth of each month. Say the rosary daily. Pray for peace and an end to the war." There was a clap of thunder and the Lady disappeared.

On the thirteenth day of every month, the children returned to the Cova. Each time a larger crowd came with them. The story of the visions spread.

October 13 was to be the Lady's last visit, and 70,000 people crowded into Fatima. They brought their sick and their crippled, hoping for a miracle. The day before it had started to rain. The Cova turned into a sea of mud. The crowds held up umbrellas trying to keep dry.

At noon Lucia shouted, "Kneel down, Francisco and

Jacinta! I see the Lady!" At that moment the rain stopped. Everyone put away their umbrellas and fell to their knees.

A great flash split the sky. Then the Lady spoke. She said, "I am the Lady of the Rosary. People must recite the rosary every day. They must ask God's forgiveness and not offend him any more." Then she added, "I want a church built in this place to honor me."

Everyone fell to the ground in terror. The sun in many colors whirled above their heads, dancing up and down. Then it appeared to fall from the sky. Many thought it was the end of the world.

Finally the sun returned to its normal place in the sky. The thousands of wet pilgrims found their clothes had dried. Also, many who were lame could walk, the blind could see. Everyone told their neighbors about the Miracle of the Sun at Fatima. The amazing story spread around the world by telegraph and telephone.

In 1918, World War I finally ended and peace was restored. A year later a terrible epidemic swept across Europe. Jacinta and Francisco died of the flu and Lucia entered a convent. She was asked to write about everything that had happened in Fatima.

A huge church, called a basilica, was built where the Virgin Mary appeared to the three children. Thousands of people began to visit Fatima every year. Over the years, many miracles have been attributed to Our Lady of Fatima.

On May 13, 2000, Francisco and Jacinta were declared Blessed by Pope John Paul II. They are in heaven just as the Lady had predicted. Lucia dos Santos, who became a Carmelite nun, spent her long life bringing honor to the Virgin Mary who became known all over the world as Our Lady of Fatima.

Litany of the Blessed Virgin Mary

Lord, have mercy,
Christ, have mercy,
Lord, have mercy.
Christ, hear us.
Christ, graciously hear us.
God, the Father of heaven, have mercy on us.
God, the Son, Redeemer of the world,
    have mercy on us.
God, the Holy Spirit, have mercy on us.
Holy Trinity, one God, have mercy on us.
Holy Mary,
(after each invocation, respond with, "Pray for us")
                              -Pray for us.

Holy Mother of God,
Holy Virgin of virgins,
Mother of Christ,
Mother, full of grace,
Mother most pure,
Mother most chaste,
Immaculate Mother,
Sinless Mother,
Lovable Mother,

Model of mothers,

Mother of good counsel,

Mother of our Maker,

Mother of our Savior,

Wisest of virgins,

Holiest of virgins,

Virgin, powerful in the sight of God,

Virgin, merciful to us sinners,

Virgin, faithful to all God asks of you,

Mirror of holiness,

Seat of wisdom,

Cause of our joy,

Shrine of the Spirit,

Honor of your people,

Devoted handmaid of the Lord,

Mystical Rose,

Tower of David,

Tower of ivory,

House of gold,

Ark of the covenant,

Gate of heaven,

Star of hope,

Health of the sick,

Refuge of sinners,

Comfort of the afflicted,

Help of Christians,

Queen of angels,

Queen of patriarchs,

Queen of prophets,

Queen of apostles,

Queen of martyrs,

Queen of confessors,

Queen of virgins,

Queen of all saints,

Queen conceived in holiness,

Queen raised up to glory,

Queen of the Rosary,

Queen of peace,

Lamb of God, you take away the sins
    of the world, – Spare us, O Lord.

Lamb of God, you take away the sins
   of the world,
         – Graciously hear us, O Lord.
Lamb of God, you take away the sins
   of the world, – Have mercy on us.
Pray for us, O holy Mother of God,
      – That we may be made worthy
            of the promises of Christ.

Let us pray.

Lord God,
   give to your people the joy of
   continual health in mind and body.

With the prayers of the Virgin Mary
   to help us, guide us through
   the sorrows of this life to
   eternal happiness in the life to come.

We ask this through Christ our Lord.   Amen.